NOT MAN APART

It is only a little planet
But how beautiful it is.

Wynn Bullock: *Sunset, Big Sur country*

Water that owns the north and west and south
And is all colors and never is all quiet,

CEDRIC WRIGHT: *Pacific*

And the fogs are its breath . . .

STEVE CROUCH: *Fog and ridges below Big Sur*

All the free companies of windy grasses . . .

EDWARD WESTON: *Grasses and Pacific*

pure naked rock . . .

EDWARD WESTON: *Eroded rock*

. . . A lonely clearing;
    a little field of corn by the streamside;
    a roof under spared trees.

MORLEY BAER: *House, Garapata Creek*

EDWARD WESTON: *Cypress*

Love that, not man apart from that . . .

Not Man Apart

lines from ROBINSON JEFFERS

Photographs of the Big Sur Coast

by Ansel Adams, Morley Baer, Wynn Bullock,
Steve Crouch, William E. Garnett, Philip Hyde,
Eliot Porter, Cole Weston, Edward Weston,
Don Worth, Cedric Wright, and others

EDITED BY DAVID BROWER

Sierra Club • *San Francisco*

Then what is the answer?—Not to be deluded by dreams.
To know that great civilizations have broken down into violence,
　　and their tyrants come, many times before.
When open violence appears, to avoid it with honor or choose
　　the least ugly faction; these evils are essential.
To keep one's own integrity, be merciful and uncorrupted
　　and not wish for evil; and not be duped
By dreams of universal justice or happiness. These dreams will
　　not be fulfilled.
To know this, and know that however ugly the parts appear
　　the whole remains beautiful. A severed hand
Is an ugly thing, and man dissevered from the earth and stars
　　and his history . . . for contemplation or in fact . . .
Often appears atrociously ugly. Integrity is wholeness,
　　the greatest beauty is
Organic wholeness, the wholeness of life and things, the divine beauty
　　of the universe. Love that, not man
Apart from that, or else you will share man's pitiful confusions,
　　or drown in despair when his days darken.

Publisher's Note: The book is set in Fairfield, with Centaur and Arrighi display faces, by Gillick Press, Berkeley, California, lithographed on Kimberly Clark Lithofect Gloss by Barnes Press, New York City. It is bound in Columbia Sampson linen by Sendor Bindery, New York City. The design is by David Brower.

The Sierra Club, founded in 1892 by John Muir, has devoted itself to the study and protection of the nation's scenic and ecological resources—mountains, wetlands, woodlands, wild shores and rivers. All Club publications are part of the nonprofit effort the Club carries on as a public trust. There are more than 50 chapters coast to coast, in Canada, Hawaii and Alaska. Participation is invited in the Club's program to enjoy and preserve wilderness everywhere. Address: 1050 Mills Tower, San Francisco, California 94104.

Edward Weston: *Eroded rock, Point Lobos*

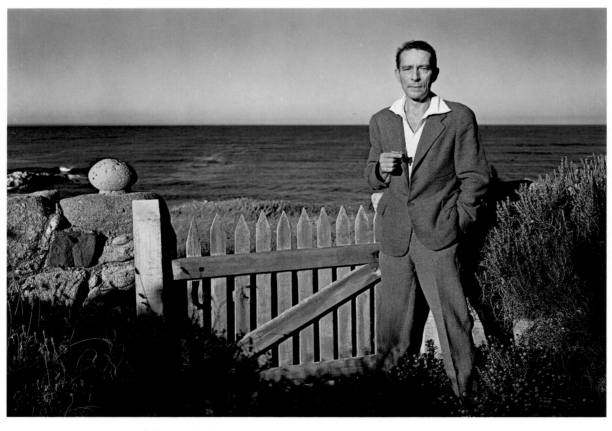

Ansel Adams: *Robinson Jeffers*

Foreword

More than thirty years ago, accompanied by Edward Weston, I met and spoke with Robinson Jeffers on the road beyond his door. The circumstances have long faded from my mind except for the haunting presence of his features, lined and immobile as a Greek mask. I have also a rough memory that he spoke casually and without heat, of being called for jury duty in a homicide case, and of having been rejected by the defense because of the assumed cruelty of his countenance. The eyes looked at me side-long as he spoke, not with amusement, but with the remote, almost inhuman animal contemplation that marks his work and that very obviously had aroused the mistaken animus of the defense counsel.

I felt in his presence almost as if I stood before another and nobler species of man whose moods and ways would remain as inscrutable to me as the ways of the invading Cro-Magnons must have seemed dark to the vanishing Neanderthals. In later and more mature years I have met cleverer vocalizers and more ingenious intellects, but I have never again encountered a man who, in one brief meeting, left me with so strong an impression that I had been speaking with someone out of time, an oracle who would presently withdraw among the nearby stones and pinewood.

A yearning for that retreat can be felt in Jeffers' work. D. H. Lawrence once observed that the essence of poetry "is stark direct-ness, without a shadow of a lie, or a shadow of deflection any-where." No one reading Jeffers can escape the impress of the untamed Pacific environment upon which he brooded. He was its most powerful embodiment — an incarnation of the spirit of place so intense as to epitomize Lawrence's demand that there be no deflection between the poet and what he expresses. Jeffers' peculiarly distinctive style, developed by degrees from the un-promising conventional prosody of his youth, has the roll of surf and the jaggedness of rocks about it. Something utterly wild had crept into his mind and marked his features. I cannot imagine him as having arisen unchanged in another countryside. The sea-beaten coast, the fierce freedom of its hunting hawks, possessed and spoke through him. It was one of the most uncanny and com-plete relationships between and man and his natural background that I know in literature. It tells us something of the power of the western landscape here at world's end where the last of the Ameri-can dream turned inward upon itself.

Jeffers was not limited to the simple expression of the natural. Fierce shapes and dark symbols, as intimidating as certain super-natural evocations in his long narratives, erupt from even his short poems. He was an educated man whose mind roved from the contemplation of nebulae to the incipient beginnings of planetary life. He felt in his bones man's transcience and the looming disaster contained in the sciences upon which man placed his hope. Stones, the bones of deer, Indian palm prints in a cave—all relate themselves symbolically to us but remind us at the same time of our human mortality.

Man himself will descend into the night he has decreed for other creatures. His untidy lunch boxes, his defilement of beaches will eventually, in some oncoming age, disappear before the great winter storms of the Pacific. Musing upon the rusted machinery in an abandoned stone quarry, Jeffers notes the persistent intru-sion of expelled nature: "Men's failures are often as beautiful as men's triumphs but your returnings/are even more precious than your first presence."

With an artist's eye he has seen how quickly ugly ruins perched upon by birds and subjected to the weather can be trans-muted and softened into beauty. He observes that a similar but lost nobility would return to man if he could but regain "the dignity of rareness." Of an old rancher who had spent his life under the open sky, Jeffers remarked that his was an existence all of our ancestors since the ice age would have known and appreciated.

With a kind of austere Spenglerian aloofness, "a neutral among all the dreaming factions," the poet looked on without hope for man, but at the same time he remained touchingly sensitive to individual tragedy whether animal or human. A person of great emotional depth, he suffered as only the seer can suffer in an age of vulgarity and material affluence. The Pacific at his door-step became for Jeffers an enormous blue eyeball staring into outer space, staring perhaps into that "hawk's-dream future" which now is almost an obsession with humanity. Men feel, in growing numbers, the drawing of a net of dependency against which something wild in their natures still struggles as desperately as trapped fish in a seine. They ride in imagination with the astronauts, yearning for the last crag "on the ocean of the far stars." "No escape," counters Jeffers:

> "I feel the steep time build like a wave,
>   towering to break...."

The poet is not unaware at times of those elemental forces which speak through him. In a moment of self-critical understatement he remarks: "It is certain you have loved the beauty of storm disproportionately."

The man saw correctly. His long narratives threaded with violence made him a cult object in the twenties and early thirties so that to reread the critical effusions about him causes one to blush a little for the extravagances of the professional reviewers. Time has eroded this superficial praise and left exposed what was best in the man. Much of it will be found in the short lyrics or interpolated in the narratives. The best passages will be found concerned with waves and sea-fog, the small hoof-prints of deer, the clay homes of swallows under the eaves, the passages of hawks or mountain lions—all, that up to our time, has been re-garded as permanent in the American landscape.

Like Thoreau, Jeffers was essentially solitary in his communion with nature. Both men were profoundly "imprinted," as the mod-ern biologist would say, with their natural environment. It meant more to them than their human surroundings and they drew their literary sustenance from it. The one, Jeffers, is more addicted to the surge of the great waters, the other to a New England winter reserve. Both, though separated by a century as well as a continent, express the frontiersmen's distaste for numbers. Jeffers eyes the sea birds "alone in a nihilist simplicity." Thoreau con-fesses "an immense appetite for solitude," and maintains that he never met any man so elevating as the silence of a meadow.

Somewhat like Jeffers before the abandoned rock quarry, Thoreau sensed the aroma arising from ruined nature: "It is not in vain, perhaps, that every winter the forest is brought to our doors, shaggy with lichens. Even in so humble a shape as the wood-pile, it contains sermons for us." As Jeffers, later, was to examine the palm prints of an exterminated race on a cave wall, Thoreau is attracted by the arrow heads "sleeping in the skin of the revolving earth." He calls them "fossil thoughts" which will outlast today's sculptures. Similarly, in a letter addressed to me in the thirties, Jeffers expressed a fascinated interest in the Folsom and Yuma archaeological discoveries which were then beginning to suggest an unexpected ice-age antiquity for man in the New World.

With Jeffers, however, the American wilderness is dangerously close to sundown. One is forced to turn and survey the cities on the site of vanished forests, the vast population explosion with its dire implications, the two great decimating wars of our century and, finally, the nature of man himself—or such intimations as earth's strata choose to reveal, perhaps in those same arrow points. Jeffers recognizes that we have treated America's prodigal riches, not with love, but as despoilers. Within a few generations we have destroyed our forests, and mutilated the landscape almost beyond recall. A powerful sense of alienation has turned our literature to cracked laughter and pornography. The sound mind seeks to be "laired in the rock that sheds pleasure and pain like hailstones."

Thoreau tried hard to get his head above the clouds that represented "the underside of heaven's pavement." He was convinced that we had not got half way to dawn and he laid down, for a recluse, some rather discerning precepts for getting there. They included, among other things, a preservation of wilderness as necessary for the well-being and preservation of man.

Over three hundred years ago another poet and mystic, Thomas Trahearne, who looked almost as sadly upon man as Jeffers, wrote: "There are invisible ways of conveyance by which some great thing doth touch our souls." For Americans, those ways of insight have, throughout our history, lain mostly in a profound reaction to the natural world about us, a deep transfusion, "a conveyance" of life, or wonder, found under the forest roof and in the great solitudes of the new continent. Jeffers, well read in the sciences, extended that wilderness to sidereal space:

> "desperate wee galaxies…shining
>   their substance away like a passionate
>   thought."

Jeffers never succeeded very well in immuring his mind in the stone house he loved. The "unagitable" nature in which he tried to clothe himself shrank perceptibly before the brutalities of the hunter, the axmen and the forest burners. He speaks bitterly of the starving sea bird on the strand, its feathers befouled with oil, or of the sea lion blinded by human thoughtlessness and malice.

"My essence was capacity," Trahearne wrote. The comment might have served as Jeffers' epitaph. Bird, man, and star were transcended in his search for that organic wholeness which he prayed for, and which eluded him.

Part of him could be said to lie in the photographs of this book, or rather, they mark his passage. Pictured are his beloved cypress worked into knots by "the sailor wind," the great raptor birds, diminishing, untamable, as man and the cities spread. There are the nebulae glimpsed from Mount Palomar fleeing, as it seemed to the poet, this "center of infection," consciousness. Jeffers, in his apostrophes to the rocks he envied, or to the slow life of forest redwoods, exhibits an infinite capacity for love outside that fragment of nature we call humanity. He saw humanity as the destroyer of a world it could not live without and remain human. He pleads with us to be, not fractional, but whole men; partakers and enjoyers of the natural world outside ourselves, not trapped in men's "pitiful confusions." The wise, he says, seek solitude, "the splendor of inhuman things," which give value and meaning to our lives.

Jeffers is gone now, and so many years and miles lie between us that I do not care to ask the fate of the trees he loved to plant, nor of those who stood with us on that summer afternoon at Carmel. I suppose, a century after Thoreau and being the man he was, Jeffers would have doubted we were half way to dawn or even that dawn would come.

As I look at these pictures drawn at random from the world he loved, it is not at the end the brutal male figures with their magnified human cruelty that cross the rock-torn stage. Now in my late years all those fierce voices have passed unremembered from my mind. What remains to me are the lines from *The Loving Shepherdess:*

> "All our pain comes from restraint of love…
>   The beetle beside my hand in the grass
>   and the little brown bird tilted on a stone…
>   there was nothing there that I didn't love with my heart…"

I, who spent much time alone in my young years, and who, out of sheer love of life, planted sapling trees that were destined mostly to be torn up, am not unfamiliar with such feelings. I choose to remember this gentler aspect of Jeffers.

Clare Walker's love, driven mad by tragedy, had been extended beyond human boundaries. Her compassion for life was so intense that she became life's victim. Perhaps Jeffers meant to show this, but, in reality, this lost girl of the roadside, walking with her faithful sheep through rain and hunger, to death, is the most agonizingly real of Jeffers' characters. Dying, she dwarfs "normal" humanity. Psychologically unfit though she is pictured, I suspect that something escaped the reserved Jeffers that he did not quite intend. "Love the coast opposite humanity and so be freed," he had once written gruffly. But the loving shepherdess had come by way of loss to Trahearne's magnificent insight: "The more we live in all, the more we live in one."

Since, to my mind, the shepherdess is actually the alter-ego of Jeffers, it is evident that he who found it difficult to bear the sight of laboratory animals had his own experience of compassion. "Sane men," he writes ironically of the experimenters, "well buttoned in their own skins." He does not praise them, though they are insulated from pity, laired truly in the rock of insensitivity that he professes to long for. Instead, he cried with a sudden anguish that might have been torn from Clare Walker:

> "whilst I like a dowser go here and there
>   with skinless pity for the dipping hazel fork."

Thus Jeffers confronts the paradox of his daemon: to escape and not to love; to love and not escape. I think Clare Walker's was the nobler folly. I think, at heart, her creator knew this. The man who had confessed to "widening the disastrous consciousness of life with poems," projected through another mask than his own the agony of that love which encompasses both man and his creatures.

Robinson Jeffers had endured the all in the one, known the infinite capacity for love which makes man so pitiably vulnerable, as was true of his last years. I do not know where he lies, but something of his insights and perceptions may linger in these pages in such a manner as to intrigue a later generation. I hope so, for his mind was deeply sensitive to those aspects of nature which contribute to the creation and maintenance of human dignity, and which are sadly threatened in our time.

LOREN EISELEY

Wynnewood, Pennsylvania
June 10, 1965

Preface

The Jeffers country is fully qualified, if any place is, to be a national seashore in perpetuity, but it never will be—not in the usual sense. The national approach that seems to be working along the Ocean Strip of the Olympic Peninsula, or at Point Reyes, or at Capes Cod and Hatteras, or on Fire Island, is not likely to work between Point Lobos and Piedras Blancas—the Big Sur Coast.

If the traditional approach to preservation won't work for this, one of the great meetings of wild ocean and almost-wild coast, then what can be done to make sure it will remain a great place? We need to find out and *Not Man Apart* may play a role in the search. We hope also that it will remind those who already know it how splendid a place it is, or will bring an intimation of that splendor to those who have never been there, encouraging them, not too many at a time, to seek it out.

If they do and their spirits are not moved by it, they cannot help. Those who are moved, we would like to think, will somehow see that the significant things on this coastline endure; it was John Muir's postulate seventy-three years ago that those who know a place well can defend it best and we still think so. In the Club he founded we still try to make as secure as we can—by enlisting public assistance—those exhibits of wildness where the evolutionary force, the life force, has come down through the ages unbroken in its essence by man and his technology. We are concerned about this continuity in areas already dedicated by various agencies of government. We are also concerned about places, growing ever rarer, that are still wilderness in fact even though the government has not yet been persuaded to set them aside.

We give high priority to wilderness because it is the most fragile resource: man can destroy but not create it. Whoever would rescue wilderness, we have also learned, must watch his point of view. The threshold he steps into wilderness from, or the frame he looks into it through, is also important, and we concern ourselves with both. We believe that neither will be safe unless it can be demonstrated that both will serve man. Other creatures have a right to a place in the sun, whether or not man be there, but they have no standing in court and no vote with which to defend themselves against technology. We try to vote in their behalf, now and then, and for the wildness that they cannot live without. We and several organizations like us welcome the assistance of citizens who, like Aldo Leopold, cannot live without wildness either.

* * * * *

What is wilder than the Pacific? An occasional ship passes by, but its wake closes quickly, emphasizing the wildness. The foreground, however, may do something else; it can destroy the mood of a far-off horizon.

Through what frame do you look at your Pacific? Do you look across the backyard of people who were thinking something else when they dumped their garbage down the cliff in their own backyard, spewed it over the miraculous rock gardens, tossed it into the surge of surf, where an old shoe now floats among the waving sea palms? I saw this once on a cove where an elite could put up their houses and fences and preëmpt the vantage points. If you were lucky yourself, if you got there first

and could afford it, you actually own the frame and see to it that few intrude upon the solitude that was so hard to find. If you are less lucky, came later, and have to skimp, you may have no frame at all.

Whoever you are, the ocean wildness that confronts you in the few places a beach is open to you may be so new, so all-encompassing, so limitless that you haven't thought about its rarity or its jeopardy. In your once-in-a-year seaside weekend the beach-fire embers can easily be left, the beer enjoyed fully and the cans tossed, the bottles caromed off the sea-worn stone, the razor edges left to last almost forever underfoot. The wild bird is a moving target to be shot at (try to explain to your child why the gull that just soared so gracefully in the sea wind now lies dead in the surf—because some kid didn't think about what his .22 was doing). It doesn't seem to matter. Here is freedom, space, the wild world you can still move in, not so crowded you need permission to run or throw or shoot. You do what you wouldn't do had you thought about the speed with which man is diminishing wildness, no matter what his income bracket.

It doesn't take much conjecturing to understand the resenting of people by one group and of fences by another. Perhaps we can avoid a stalemate by looking into what England has learned. There, in favorite places, the British could establish national parks of a special kind, to serve people and to respect a place, made available by people who happened to own it, who happened to love it and the things that belong in it, the tough and the fragile. They let you in if you will share their emotional attachment for it, if you will contribute toward what it takes to keep the place intact, if you will close the gate behind you when you enter to enjoy and when you leave to remember.

We could use this approach. We are fast running out of the great expanses of original wilderness that can be preserved by government. We still have many places privately owned, protected by sensitive people now—but soon bound to be broken up as their own lives break or end. These are places we love, or that our children may come to love if we leave them the chance; and they are places we are not finding it possible to buy or to vote protection for.

We can still try to purchase preservation. Meanwhile, or instead, we can borrow from the British. They borrowed the national park concept from us. We can now learn from them. Nathaniel Owings is one man who has already learned and who has added refinements the British may borrow back and refine further. His chief allies were Fred Farr, a member of the California Senate; Tom Hudson, a Monterey County Supervisor; and Nicholas Roosevelt, who lives high up on Partington Ridge and is genetically a conservationist. Assuming that there was bound to be development now that the Coast road had been built and improved, they wondered if that development might strive to augment the natural beauty of the coast, not clobber it.

What are the priorities? For the highway traveler as well as the resident, the seascape comes first; it must be kept uncluttered, or the clutter removed soon. The sense of openness, the wild sweep of ridges from the Santa Lucias to the sea, is almost equally important. These things come first because they affect so many people—those who drive by and who can only pause, not linger.

But on this, one of the most remarkable coasts of all, there must also be something lasting for those who would linger. Astride the highway is wilderness that should be kept intact. It belongs to everyone who drives the highway whether or not he owns it, whether he climbs to run its ridges or descends to walk its beaches. It is wild and he knows it is *his,* as all wildness is everyone's—something everyone can delight in, knowing that there are still good places where man has the sense to leave things alone, letting the forces that created them keep on creating.

How, then, to let man's works lie lightly on the land, in pools of development, not in an all-pervading drizzle. How to avoid the usual slash and spill, with a slab to mark the spot where beauty died? Can architecture respect the slope that is there? Can the ever-changing chaparral itself be spared and not supplanted with a scooped-out terrace begreened in clichés? Can one part of a house be high and another low because that's the way the land lies? Can houses be clustered, mindful of man's built-in need for at least some congregating, leaving broad spaces open to fulfill still another need? And can the seascape be kept clear?

Imaginative architecture and landscaping can help; so can zoning; so can the separation of development rights and scenic easements from the ownership of the surface itself; so can sensible innovation in taxation, with the public giving an advantage to the owner who gives the public an advantage. Later there may need to be some further governmental ownership of places that get the greatest public impact—even as the British are now

finding it necessary to do. There can be established by law a body representative of various kinds of landowners, private and public, cognizant of the integrity of the whole stretch of coast and its back country and empowered to act in its behalf.

A better course may appear, but here is something to aim at, and Nathaniel Owings has supplied the creative force and dynamic effort it took to make a start. He and his associates sought out the best man might do with an environment he wants to live in as well as preserve. Private owners might yet join forces with the Forest Service, which manages the wilderness and recreational lands in the area, with the Defense Department and its inland reservation and coastal installations, with the State and its parks, and with the Division of Highways, challenged here to move people but not mountains. Pico Blanco might still remain as uniquely beautiful as it was to Jeffers and not be reduced by the removal of its common limestone. A dramatic system of coastal ridges could be encompassed in a Ventana Wilderness established under the provisions of the new Wilderness Act.

The choice is still open. The Big Sur Coast can be the place where, from here on out, man asks not what he can do to hurt the earth, but what to do so as not to hurt it but to achieve restraint instead, leaving marks that are faint, or that aren't there at all.

DAVID BROWER

San Francisco, May 19, 1965

Acknowledgments

The idea of blending photographs with lines from Robinson Jeffers is not new. Jeffers himself tells here of Horace Lyon's proposal that never materialized. Francis Farquhar, in the 1933 *Sierra Club Bulletin,* illustrated lines from *Tamar* with a photograph by Ansel Adams (we have used Edward Weston for those lines and Adams for others). Nancy Newhall prepared a presentation for *Life,* using Weston's photographs; some of her apposition has found its way into this book. I tried my hand with some photographs of Philip Hyde's in the 1961 *Bulletin,* having a book in mind and not knowing that anyone else did. It was Mrs. Newhall, in *This Is the American Earth,* who unknowingly started me. She had augmented Cedric Wright's photograph of a fawn with four lines from *The Bloody Sire* that stayed with me:

> What but the wolf's tooth whittled so fine
> The fleet limbs of the antelope?
> What but fear winged the birds, and hunger
> Jewelled with such eyes the great goshawk's head?

I myself wanted to experiment with the words of the man who could compress so much understanding so beautifully, but other obligations kept getting in the way.

At the critical time and over the course of a year, Lewis Ellingham made a major contribution. Nancy Newhall passed to him the work she had started, he went through the works of Jeffers carefully and also through much of the work of most of the photographers represented here. He was in touch with the Jeffers family and many other Jeffers experts, with photographers, with painters, with people who lived in the country. From his poetic instincts and creative drive the beginnings of a book evolved

that would serve the art of poetry well and that would present Jeffers well too, in an admirable anthology illustrated with photographs of the Big Sur country.

But because Sierra Club books have their own peculiar purpose, we were not ready for this combination but needed the opposite—the country itself, its meaning reinforced by Jeffers, the whole greater than the sum of its parts. We could agree with Jeffers that man should "uncenter his mind from humanity," but would have to disagree about how far to uncenter. We could not stress that part of Jeffers that preached inhumanism—or that seemed to, in superficial reading. It could not be our role to contemplate death as passionately as some of his poems do, nor to accentuate images that come to mind more readily than tongue. Other publishers could handle this well; we could not. We could go along with the belief that man's total concern with himself and his technology is not healthy and should be tempered with a little love and respect for wholeness. We could try to take Jeffers' prediction of human destruction as a challenge and try to prove him wrong—in our program but not in the book. We could go, though, to the British again for another attitude—a willingness to avoid trying "to sum it all up" in a book, we could try to make an interesting book, not one that pretends by any means to have got the whole truth, either from our own files on policy or from an oracle. Surely we needed one that could reflect in its photographic beauty the coast it ought to celebrate and that Jeffers certainly did.

In the course of all this a temporary postman happened by the house to bring us a letter from Ansel Adams and to remark that he had just heard about our Jeffers book down in Carmel. One conversation led to several, and to the revelation that he was a walking concordance to Jeffers; he not only knew the lines but was also seeking out the specific places the lines were about. We were missing important things, he said, and in between special-delivery errands he wrote out instructions, based upon his own extraordinary collection of Jeffersiana, about where we should look.

We needed to go back through Jeffers and the photographs to restructure the book completely, to exploit the advice of Wallace Stegner and Ansel Adams, the members of the club's Publications Committee who could best help us combine poetry, photography, and coast. The young man who now took on this task should have his name on the title page because we owe him more than anyone else this book's survival. But he refused and my name is on the title page instead. This will give indexers and bibliographers a hook to hang on, and it is a project that I started the club on, switched in midstream, designed, devised some of the photographic sequences for and assumed responsibility for seeking and rejecting help, and so on.

The book owes much to many. Our gratitude encompasses many kinds of endeavor. For the pattern, for exploiting the equivalent, as Alfred Stieglitz called it, we thank Ansel Adams and Nancy Newhall, who launched the series of exhibit-format books. We thank all the photographers and other artists whose work we include and those we could not include but who by contributing raised the entire level of selection.

For the assistance they gave Lewis Ellingham we are grateful to Melba Berry Bennett, Professors Frederic Ives Carpenter and James D. Hart, Robert Duncan, Horace Lyon, Neil Weston, Dr. Hamilton Jeffers, Donnan and Garth Jeffers, and Father Robert J. Brophy, S.J., who prepared an invaluable bibliography of the works of Jeffers.

As the project developed, we drew upon advice, generously given, from Lawrence Clark Powell, David Magee, Marlan Beilke, David Hales, Nathaniel Owings and Margaret Wentworth Owings. We acknowledge the very kind offer to assist that was extended by Radcliffe Squires, and wish things had been ordered enough at the time for us to exploit what he knows of Jeffers.

In the final shaping the book had invaluable help from George Marshall, Professor Wallace Stegner, and again from Ansel Adams and Virginia Adams, in the coördination of the search for photographs.

For financial assistance we are grateful to the Foundation for Environmental Design for a grant that helped build faith when it was needed, and we are further grateful to the many givers of modest contributions "with no strings," who cast bread upon the waters to launch this book, in turn to help other books in causes that we hope can be well served.

For supplementary help on illustrations we thank Mrs. Cedric Wright; the Archaeological Research Facility, University of California, Berkeley; Dr. Albert Whitford, Director of the University's Lick Observatory, Mount Hamilton; the Museum of Modern Art and the Wenner-Gren Foundation; and Tyrus G. Harmsen and the Occidental College Robinson Jeffers collection. The plunging hawk of the endpapers is the work of Margaret Owings.

The Jeffers material itself is published through the kind permission of Random House, Donnan Jeffers, and Horace Lyon. Anyone wishing to know more about Father Brophy's bibliography or about what has become known as the Owings Plan for the Big Sur coast—the plan alluded to in the Preface and Introduction—should address the Sierra Club.

For all their inadequacy, short acknowledgments are at least safe. When so many have contributed, the chances of oversight are frightening. For all I have omitted I ask forgiveness. Penultimately I must thank my wife, Anne, an editor herself, for the gentleness and the firmness of her counsel about what was going on throughout the course of the creative process. As always, she could discern the soft spots far in advance of my getting hopelessly mired in them.

Finally I am grateful to the young man whose name, as I said, should be on the title page—my oldest son, Kenneth Brower. He loves the Big Sur coast as much, I think, as his parents do. He has built some good sand castles there, he has run some of the ridges and beaches, and he didn't like it when the gull fell into the foam at his feet. We disagree now and then, but not about this coast and what it means.   D. B.

Introduction

The regret we feel for fallen leaves is seasonal, for we know about the imminent renewal of springtime. The regret stirred by the death of a landscape, however, is long lasting and singularly probes our thinking; we may well wonder whether we have taken the immobility of stone too much for granted.

We have taken for granted for more than a century the rocky coastlands of the Santa Lucias down the Big Sur Coast. We assumed that Rancho San José y Sur Chiquito would always stretch south from Point Lobos as a permanent pasture, edged with some twenty-five miles of shoreline, radiant green in spring, often veiled in fog, parched to gold in summer. There was an inviolable quality to the shore which suggested a birthright for all the people.

Farther south was a grant received from the Spanish Throne in the 1830's by a whaling captain, John Bautiste Roger Cooper. This holding penetrated the deep forks of the Little Sur River, embraced the fields that rose above the mouth of the Big Sur River, and ran back into the secluded Sur Valley, where the redwood groves, the sycamore, and the clumps of wind-carved laurel grew.

Forty years passed and new settlers came, staking out their homestead and timber claims, accepting the isolation, hoping they could sustain themselves on ranches, making the most of the sloping shelves that interrupted the ridges and canyons that plunged to the sea. The Pfeiffers, the Posts, the Dani family, and the Brazils grazed cattle, tanned buckskin, raised hogs, and shipped redwood pickets and tanbark, proud of their skill in making a lonely living. They bought shoes and yardage goods as personal necessities; coffee beans, sugar, and rice as luxuries.

Their names on the mailboxes still mark the land along the road. But it is a different road. The mail delivery to Big Sur as Jeffers described it in 1914 was a dawn-to-dark excursion in a horse-drawn stage. Today it takes less than an hour. The paved road saved time, but the saving was not free. It was paid for with a corresponding loss of remote wildness. Pause for coffee in a rancher's kitchen and you may still hear of the whaling days when grizzlies crashed through the dry sycamore leaves, padding out onto the sands along the Lighthouse Flats to feast on whales washed ashore. You may still hear accounts of the herds of deer moving over the slopes at dawn, or even of the mountain lion quietly following the trail of a returning settler at dusk, a silent shadow, unmolesting.

Or you may recapture the days a hundred years ago when Francesca, the wife of Manuel Innocenti—they were the last Indian family in the valley—would walk barefoot through the woods to call on Barbara Pfeiffer at her cabin in Sycamore Canyon. These were formal calls, these meetings of two solitary women, Francesca always carrying her store shoes, stopping to put them on before she arrived. They sat in silence, one unable to speak Spanish or the Indian tongue, the other unable to speak English, communicating simply as women.

South of Big Sur there were only the sea and rugged trails. The Upper Coast Trail laboriously climbed some 3,000 feet to where black oaks, Coulter pines, and madrone topped the ridge and stood dark against the sky. Robinson Jeffers describes what happens here:

I, gazing at the boundaries of granite and spray, the
Established sea-marks, felt behind me
Mountain and plain, the immense breadth of the continent
Before me, the mass and doubled stretch of water.

The Lower Coast Trail threaded its way into redwood canyons, where deer browsed the deep walls of the running streams. It climbed the steep slopes of chaparral out onto the "lion-colored hills" spotted with yucca. The Castros, the Grimes, and the Torres built their homes along this trail and lived a life that accepts wilderness as a neighbor.

There was a rendezvous here, where seventy-two miles of wild coast country lay dazzling in the sun. Rachel Carson called such meeting "a place of compromise, conflict and eternal change." Here sea and land consorted, the seeping moisture in each fold of the mountain range emerged and slipped musically into the shifting continents of kelp. The conflict and change was a natural interplay in the balance of life. Then came the road.

The new road intruded upon a dynamic ecological balance, divided what had been the indivisibility of the living whole. The old coach road from Monterey to Big Sur, carved out by settlers in 1886, accepted the terrain, explored each canyon and scouted each ridge. By 1932 road engineers set about to stabilize, widen and shorten—and to span the deep canyon at Bixby Landing with a boldly fashioned concrete arch. South of Big Sur Valley, the road cut hard into "the hundred-fold ridges." Blocks of landscape were spilled into the redwood canyons or tumbled into the sea seven hundred feet below. Man's intrusion left erosive scars that would not heal in his time. The earth, jarred by dynamite, still seeks the balance that was, and each winter loosens the rocks that block the natural channels on the cliffs, letting a rain of slides thunder over the narrow road. Perhaps the gray fox is agile enough still to climb and descend through the new chaos; few other living things could count on a foothold—not even the chaparral.

The new road brought new settlers, writers, artists, retired or active, industrialists and soldiers who, pricking with the needle of civilization, sought here a partial exile. In their new solitude, all these people had one element in common—the background of the superb landscape.

Twenty-five years after the improved coast road was cut through, the pressures to modernize it began—to realign its curves, to build straight slices for speed that could serve a fast-traveling public—mass-recreation seekers, and the projected real-estate developers. State engineers proposed to put this road into the freeway system. To demand a straight broad freeway along these unstable cliffs was to ask for disaster—a laying waste of environment, of integrity, of natural balance, of the very quality man was willing to travel far to experience. Real-estate developments, out of harmony with the land, threatened to spread unguided down the coast from the north and up from the south, to deface the scenery with roadside buildings, with shelves bulldozed in the mountains for house sites, girdling the smooth hills with roads. They planned a phalanx of houses between the road and the sea. Some developers advocated "a reasonable space between houses along the shore," others advised "clear the land of its natural growth to prevent fires." But where, in all this, would the brodeia hills of childhood be? Where in the years to come would we find the slopes covered by blooms reflecting the sky in their petals? Where the Jeffers' fields, "veiled in a late rain, wreathed with wet poppies," awaiting spring?

* * * * *

It was in 1960 that a group of Big Sur citizens called a meeting at the Grange Hall. Recent residents joined with some of the early settlers in sensing that the mountain shoreline could remain the same only if wisdom and foresight prevented its misuse. Together they began to view their environment with a new perspective, appreciating that future plans thrust upon their country, plans that would be considered normal developments in other portions of the state, could here destroy those things they most valued. They set about to defend them.

Out of the movement grew a master plan, encompassing the full length of the south coast. Its formulators listened hard for the words of the earth. Their goal was to preserve the coast without imposing unjustifiable restrictions on landowners. It was necessary to secure a consensus in the effort to solve a dilemma—the kind of dilemma the American of the future will be facing more and more. The master plan called for clustering, for open space, for controls for future commercial developments that would be economically sound and resourceful.

As a key step, the Legislature was persuaded to remove Highway 1 from the State Freeway system. It would be instead, the "scenic highway" prototype for a concept adopted throughout California. Since the road would be inadequate if, in addition to summer tourist travel, large developments fed into it, the master plan proponents set about to control densities and draw up plans for scenic corridors. After two years of controversy, the plan was passed. Its proponents had reached high and had not achieved their highest aims but the final compromise was well worth the long struggle. In the course of the struggle we learned to face and accept new responsibilities in dealing with the land itself, to respect its fragile character, to perceive the meaning of the road.

Those of us privileged to live on this coast, in the immensity of its scope and in its great proportion, enjoy a strong sense of belonging. Perched on the buttresses of the range, we might with Sigurd Olson call them "the final bastions of the spirit of man." In our lifetime, may we thus hold them in our hearts—for the unknown date and hour of our return.

MARGARET WENTWORTH OWINGS

Big Sur, April 1965

WINGED ROCK

The flesh of the house is heavy sea-orphaned stone,
    the imagination of the house
Is in those little clay kits of swallows
Hung in the eaves, bright wings flash and return, the heavy
    rock walls commercing
With harbors of the far hills and the high
Rills of water, the river-meadow and the sea-cloud. You have also,
    O sleepy stones,
The red, the white and the marbled pigeons
To beat the blue air over the pinewood and back again
    in a moment; and the bush-hidden
Killdeer nest against the west wall-foot,
That is fed from many strange ebbs; besides the woodful
    of finches, the shoring gulls,
The sudden attentive passages of hawks.

The Sur Country

Horace Lyon told us that some of his friends had asked him, when he revisited the east after coming to live in Carmel, whether there was any such country as pictured in Jeffers' verses, or was it mere fantasy? He had assured them that it was as real as New Jersey and still they seemed skeptical; easterners are bound to think of orange groves when you speak of California; so he was going to take some photographs and show them. Perhaps he would make a little book of the photographs: if so, might he call it "Jeffers' Country"? Certainly, I said, if he wanted to. I ought to have thought of the people who really have names on this coast, because they have lived their lives in it, and their fathers before them; whilst I have only sat in its doorway and written verses about it. But the photographs meant very little to me, until I saw them.

Once seen, they stirred me to delight and enthusiasm, and sharp recognition; as in that story about Milton's daughter, when several portraits of her father were shown her and she chose one of them: "This is the very man, this is my father!" So I felt about these photographs, looking at them successively: "This is the very coast that I love, the forms and the moods, and something of the life." While I was still enjoying the pictures another thought brushed my mind. I thought of the cant we have heard about art—cant that no one has to believe in, but it seems to be generally voiced, if not accepted—that art must not be representational; it should not, if that were possible, even suggest nature; it should reject nature and produce its own forms, follow its own laws. For a moment I felt meanly suspicious: is it possible that *photography* has driven the doctrinaires into this sterile corner? Then I remembered that the same cant is recited about other arts than painting; and that even photographers have sometimes been influenced by it, so far as the honest lens would allow them. While all the while it is obvious. . . .

I dropped the thought unfinished, preferring to look through the pictures again, recognizing each scene, refreshing the emotion it had brought me, often remembering the insufficient verses through which I had tried to express the emotion. That is one reason for writing narrative poetry, and in this case a principal one: because certain scenes awake an emotion that seems to overflow the limits of lyric or description, one tries to express it in terms of human lives. Thus each of my too many stories has grown up like a plant from some particular canyon or promontory, some particular relationship of rock and water, wood, grass, and mountain. Here were photographs of their seed-plots.

I thought, 'whether the plants are good is beyond my knowledge, but certainly the garden is'; and the incidents of our first acquaintance with it came vividly to my mind. It was in December 1914, just after the world began its violent change. In those days one did not attempt the coast-road by motor; we waited in the dawn twilight for the horse-drawn mail-stage that drove twice a week to Big Sur, where the road ended then; and it was night before we arrived, and every mile of the forty had been enchanted. We, and our dog, were the only passengers on the mail-stage; we were young and in love, perhaps that contributed to the enchantment. And the coast had displayed all its winter magic for us; drifts of silver rain through great gorges, clouds dragging on the summits, storm on the rock shore, sacred calm under the redwoods.

There had already been strong storms that winter, and at Soberanes Creek the cypress trees around the farmhouse were blown to pieces. Sea-lions roared on the Lobos Rocks off shore, while the man of the house told us that last night his hundred-pound grindstone, which he kept by the back door, had been blown around the house to the front steps; here it lay. At Notley's Landing we saw the ruinous old lumber-mill (which blew down this present year, after having stood for so many) and heard the story about it. In the gorge of Mill Creek we passed under a rusted cable sagging to a stuck skip, and we were told about the lime-kilns up the canyon, cold and forgotten, with the forest growing over them. Here we changed horses, near a lonely farmhouse where an eighty-year-old man lay dying; he was dying hard, he had been dying for a week. There were forty bee-hives in rows in front of his house. On a magnificent hillside opposite a mountain-peak stood a comparatively prosperous farmhouse, apple trees behind it, and the man who lived there had killed his father with rat-poison and married his step-mother. This was the "still small music of humanity" that we heard among the mountains; there were only five or six inhabitants in forty miles, but each one had a story. We passed the little hand-hewn cabin that a man had built twenty years before and then gone up to San Francisco and been shanghaied; at last escaping the sea he came back and died here, and lay undiscovered for a month. In the cloud on top of Sur Hill a bearded old hermit met the stage, to take delivery of pilot-biscuit he had sent for. Pilot-biscuit! He had not a tooth in his head. Farther, we drove along a steep above oaks and sycamores: this was the place where a wagon loaded with drowned bodies from a shipwreck had tipped over: the bodies rolled down the slope, and it was never known whether all were gathered up again. We came down to the Sur River, and passed the albino redwood that still grows there, shining in the forest darkness, shoots of snow-white foliage growing from the stump of a lightning-struck tree: not a human story, but strange enough to be. At last we came to the farm at the end of the road, where we spent the night in a little cabin under immense redwoods. Our dog lay at the bed-foot and snarled all night long, terrified by the noises of water and the forest odors.

* * * * *

For the first time in my life I could see people living—amid magnificent unspoiled scenery—essentially as they did in the Idyls or the Sagas, or in Homer's Ithaca. Here was life purged of the ephemeral accretions. Men were riding after cattle, or plowing the headland, hovered by white sea-gulls, as they have done for thousands of years, and will for thousands of years to come. Here was contemporary life that was also permanent life, and not shut from the modern world but conscious of it and related to it, capable of expressing its spirit but unencumbered by the mass of poetically irrelevant details and complexities that make a civilization.

ROBINSON JEFFERS

[The first five paragraphs were written as a preface to a proposed book of poems and photographs; the final paragraph is an excerpt from the introduction Jeffers wrote to Selected Poems.*]*

Cole Weston: *Coast near Bixby Creek*

ANSEL ADAMS: *Big Sur coast at sunset*

Contents

TWENTY-EIGHT ILLUSTRATIONS LITHOGRAPHED IN COLOR

SOURCES

Poems marked with an asterisk are reproduced in their entirety, except for elisions indicated by ellipses; all other selections are fragments of lines or verses.

1. Invulnerable Beauty

There is this infinite energy, the power of God,
forever working — toward what purpose?

I have heard the summer dust crying to be born
As much as ever flesh cried to be quiet.

. . . thence life was born,
    Its nitrogen from ammonia, carbon from methane,
    Water from the cloud and salts from the young seas . . .

CEDRIC WRIGHT: *Clouds*

. . . the cells of life
  Bound themselves into clans, a multitude of cells
  To make one being—as the molecules before
  Had made of many one cell. Meanwhile they had invented
  Chlorophyll and ate sunlight, cradled in peace
  On the warm waves;

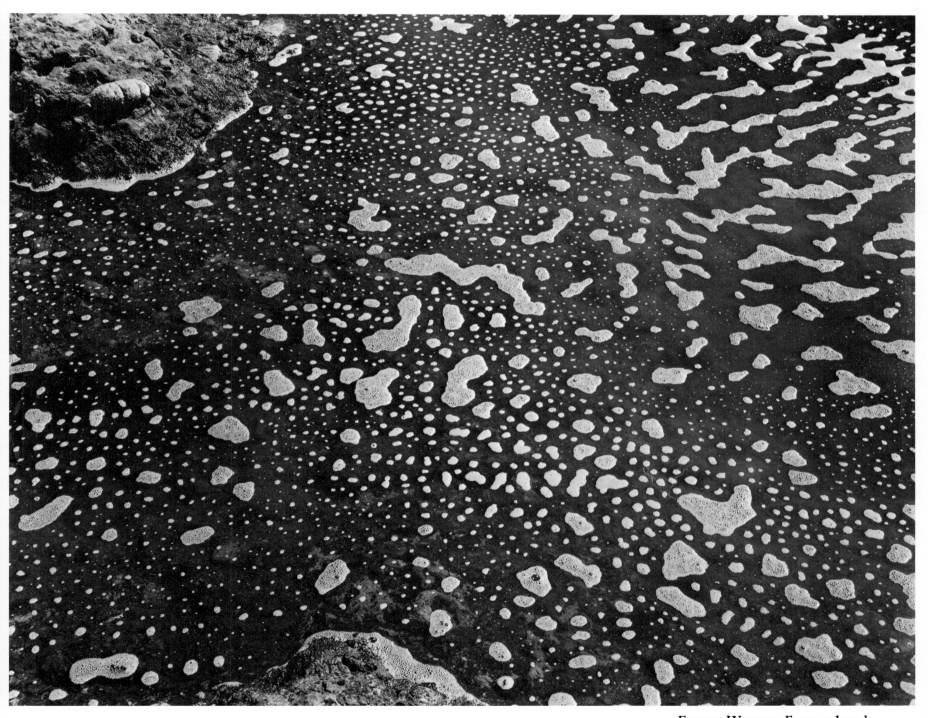

EDWARD WESTON: *Foam and sand*

> but certain assassins among them
> Discovered that it was easier to eat flesh
> Than feed on lean air and sunlight: thence the animals,
> Greedy mouths and guts, life robbing life,
> Grew from the plants; and as the ocean ebbed and
>   flowed many plants and animals
> Were stranded in the great marshes along the shore,
> Where many died and some lived. From these grew all
>   land-life,
> Plants, beasts and men; the mountain forest and the
>   mind of Aeschylus
> And the mouse in the wall.

STEVE CROUCH: *Ferns and mosses*

STEVE CROUCH: *Redwoods, Big Sur*

The beauty of things—
Is in the beholder's brain—the human mind's translation
of their transhuman
Intrinsic value.

Cole Weston: *Cabin, redwoods, and Pacific*

COLE WESTON: *Cattle grazing*

> . . . as mathematics, a human invention
> That parallels but never touches reality, gives the astronomer
> Metaphors through which he may comprehend
> The powers and the flow of things: so the human sense
> Of beauty is our metaphor of their excellence, their divine
>   nature:—like dust in a whirlwind, making
> The wild wind visible.

> . . . do you remember at all
> The beauty and strangeness of this place? Old cypresses
> The sailor wind works into deep-sea knots
> A thousand years; age-reddened granite
> That was the world's cradle . . .

PHILIP HYDE: *Shore near Point Buchon*

EDWARD WESTON:. *Cypress*

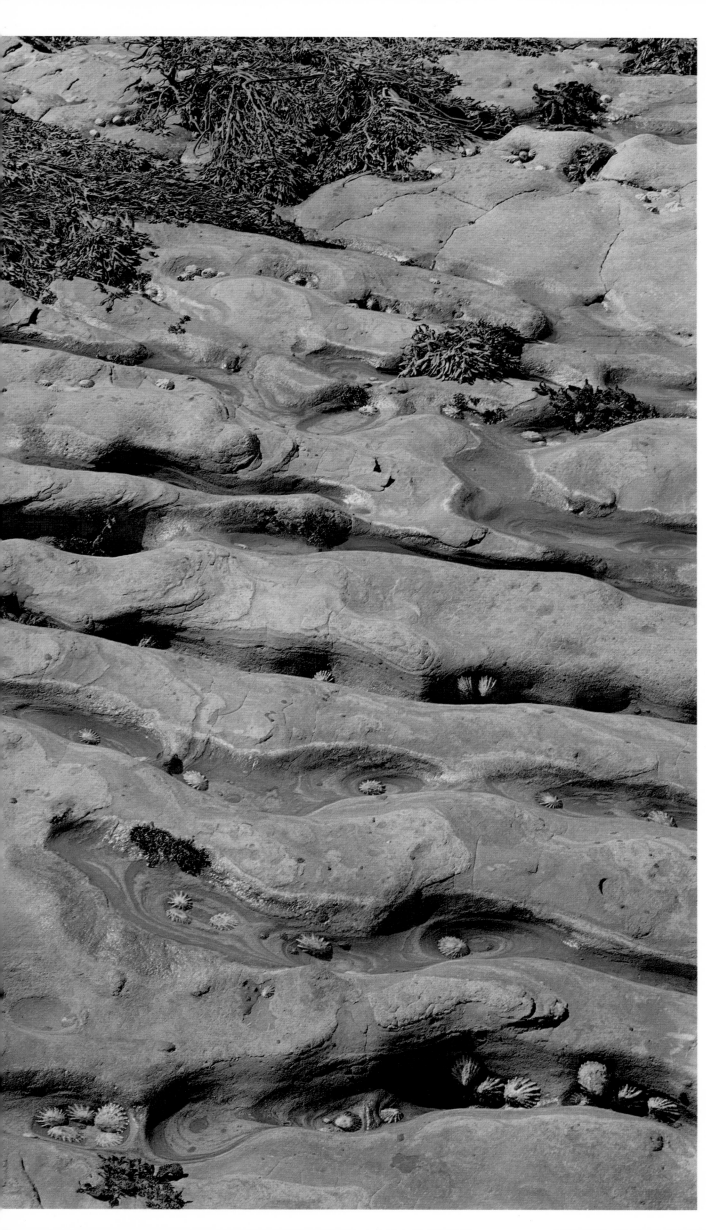

EDWARD WESTON:
Tidepools and shells

Four pelicans went over the house,
Sculled their worn oars over the courtyard: I saw that ungainliness
Magnifies the idea of strength.
A lifting gale of sea-gulls followed them; slim yachts of the element,
Natural growths of the sky, no wonder
Light wings to leave sea; but those grave weights toil,
    and are powerful,
And the wings torn with old storms remember
The cone that the oldest redwood dropped from, the tilting
    of continents,
The dinosaur's day, the lift of new sea-lines.
The omnisecular spirit keeps the old with the new also.
Nothing at all has suffered erasure.
There is life not of our time. He calls ungainly bodies
As beautiful as the grace of horses.
He is weary of nothing; he watches air-planes; he watches pelicans.

WILLIAM GARNETT: *Pelicans*

EDWARD WESTON: *Horses and ocean*

. . . And we know
        that the enormous invulnerable beauty of things
   Is the face of God, to live gladly in its presence, and die without
     grief or fear knowing it survives us.

PHILIP HYDE: *Alders at Bixby Creek*

This is God's will; he works, he grows and changes . . .

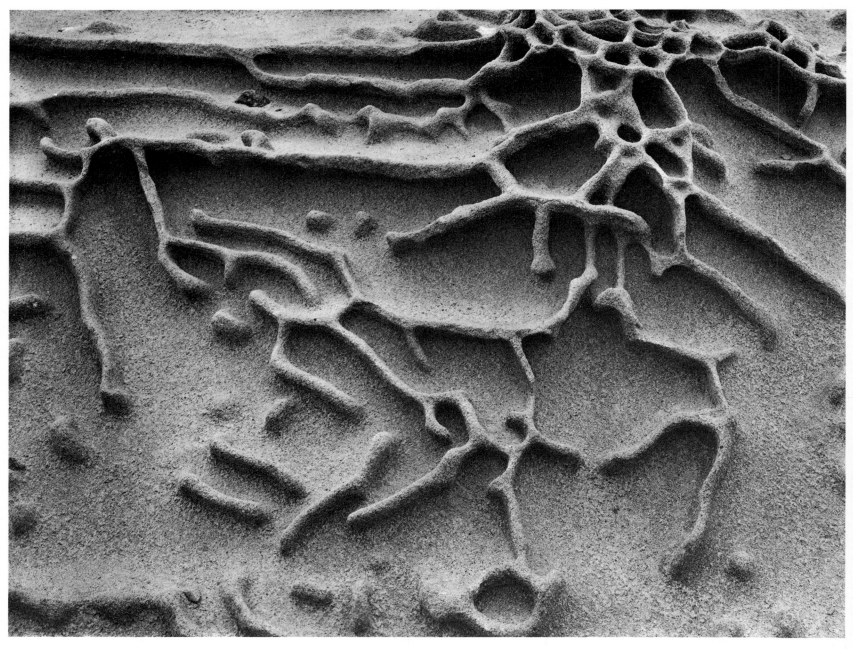

EDWARD WESTON: *Rock erosion*

PHILIP HYDE: *Ferns and Sphenopsids, Palo Colorado Canyon*

PHILIP HYDE: *Maple, Bixby Creek*

There is wind in the tree, and the
gray ocean's
Music on the rock

COLE WESTON: *Surf and rocks*

WILLIAM GARNETT: *Pfeiffer beach and hills*

PHILIP HYDE: *Point Sur from Post Road*

Here where the surf has come incredible ways out of the splendid
    west, over the deeps
Light nor life sounds forever; here where enormous sundowns flower and burn through
    color to quietness

EDWARD WESTON: *Eroded rocks, Point Lobos*

COLE WESTON: *River and beach*

. . . each November great waves awake and are drawn
Like smoking mountains bright from the west
And come and cover the cliff with white violent cleanness . . .

Like the steep necks of a herd of horses
Lined on a river margin, athirst in summer, the mountain ridges
Pitch to the sea, the lean granite-boned heads
Plunge nostril-under . . .

Cole Weston:

EDWARD WESTON: *Eroded rock, Point Lobos*

PHILIP HYDE: *Ventana Cone from Post Road*

Is it not by his high superfluousness we know
Our God? For to equal a need
Is natural, animal, mineral: but to fling
Rainbows over the rain . . .

PHILIP HYDE: *Lucia Mountains near Piedras Blancas*

And beauty above the moon, and secret rainbows
On the domes of deep sea-shells,
Not even the weeds to multiply without blossom
Nor the birds without music . . .

EDWARD WESTON: *Rock erosion, Point Lobos*

. . . Look how beautiful are all the things that He does. His
signature
Is the beauty of things.

PHILIP HYDE: *Point Lobos, south beach*

ANSEL ADAMS: *Surf*

EDWARD WESTON: *Rocks, beach and driftwood*

GRAY WEATHER

It is true that, older than man
    and ages to outlast him, the Pacific surf
Still cheerfully pounds the worn granite drum;
But there's no storm; and the birds are still,
    no song; no kind of excess;
Nothing that shines, nothing is dark;
There is neither joy nor grief nor a person,
    the sun's tooth sheathed in cloud,
And life has no more desires than a stone.
The stormy conditions of time and change
    are all abrogated, the essential
Violences of survival, pleasure,
Love, wrath and pain, and the curious desire
    of knowing, all perfectly suspended.
In the cloudy light, in the timeless quietness,
One explores deeper than the nerves
    or heart of nature, the womb or soul,
To the bone, the careless white bone, the excellence.

EDWARD WESTON: *Rocks and kelp*

. . . The rock shining dark rays and the rounded
    Crystal the ocean his beam of blackness and silence
    Edged with azure, bordered with voices . . .
    There is nothing but shines though it shine darkness; nothing but
        answers; they are caught in the net of their voices
    Though the voices be silence. . . .

. . . Whatever electron or atom or flesh or star or universe cries to me,
  Or endures in shut silence: it is my cry, my silence; I am the nerve,
    I am the agony,
  I am the endurance. . . .

EDWARD WESTON: *Stonecrop*

THE CAGED EAGLE'S DEATH DREAM

While George went to the house
For his revolver, Michal climbed up the hill
Weeping; but when he came with death in his hand
She'd not go away, but watched. At the one shot
The great dark bird leaped at the roof of the cage
In silence and struck the wood; it fell, then suddenly
Looked small and soft, muffled in its folded wings.

The nerves of men after they die dream dimly
And dwindle into their peace; they are not very passionate,
And what they had was mostly spent while they lived.
They are sieves for leaking desire; they have many pleasures
And conversations; their dreams too are like that.
The unsocial birds are a greater race;
Cold-eyed, and their blood burns. What leaped up to death,
The extension of one storm-dark wing filling its world,
Was more than the soft garment that fell. Something had flown away.
        Oh cage-hoarded desire,
Like the blade of a breaking wave reaped by the wind, or flame
        rising from fire, or cloud-coiled lightning
Suddenly unfurled in the cave of heaven: I that am stationed,
        and cold at heart, incapable of burning,
My blood like standing sea-water lapped in a stone pool,
        my desire to the rock, how can I speak of you?
Mine will go down to the deep rock.
                                This rose,
Possessing the air over its emptied prison,
The eager powers at its shoulders waving shadowless
Unwound the ever-widened spirals of flight
As a star light, it spins the night-stabbing threads
From its own strength and substance: so the aquiline desire
Burned itself into meteor freedom and spired
Higher still . . .

WILLIAM GARNETT: *Surf*

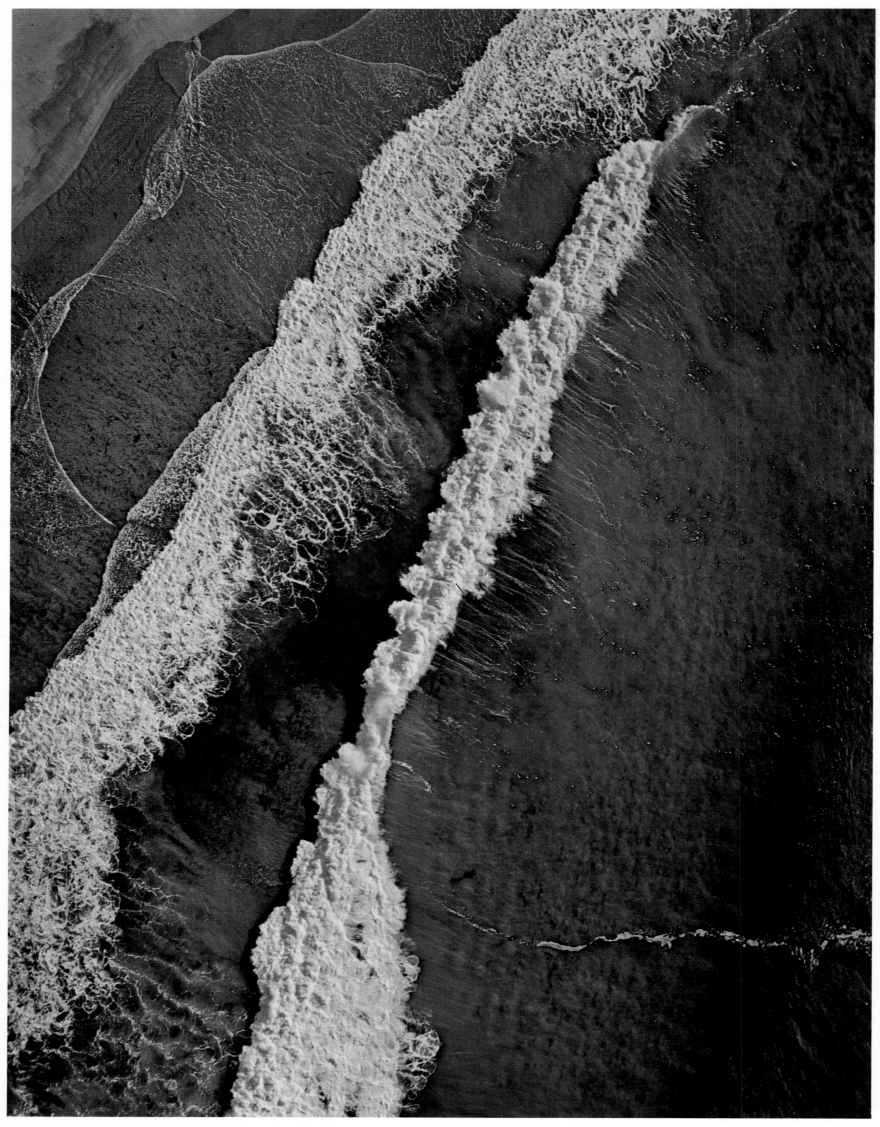

WILLIAM GARNETT: *Surf*

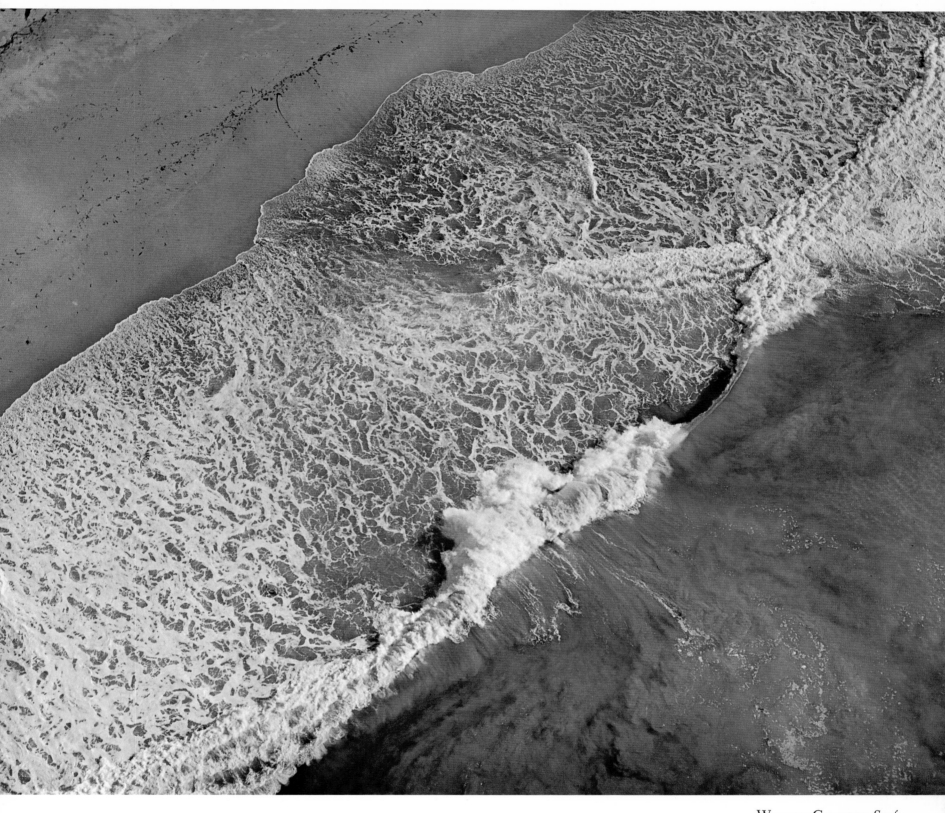

This burned and soared. The shining ocean below lay on the shore
Like the great shield of the moon come down, rolling bright rim
     to rim with the earth.

                                       Against it the multiform
And many-canyoned coast-range hills were gathered into one
                carven mountain, one modulated
Eagle's cry made stone, stopping the strength of the sea.

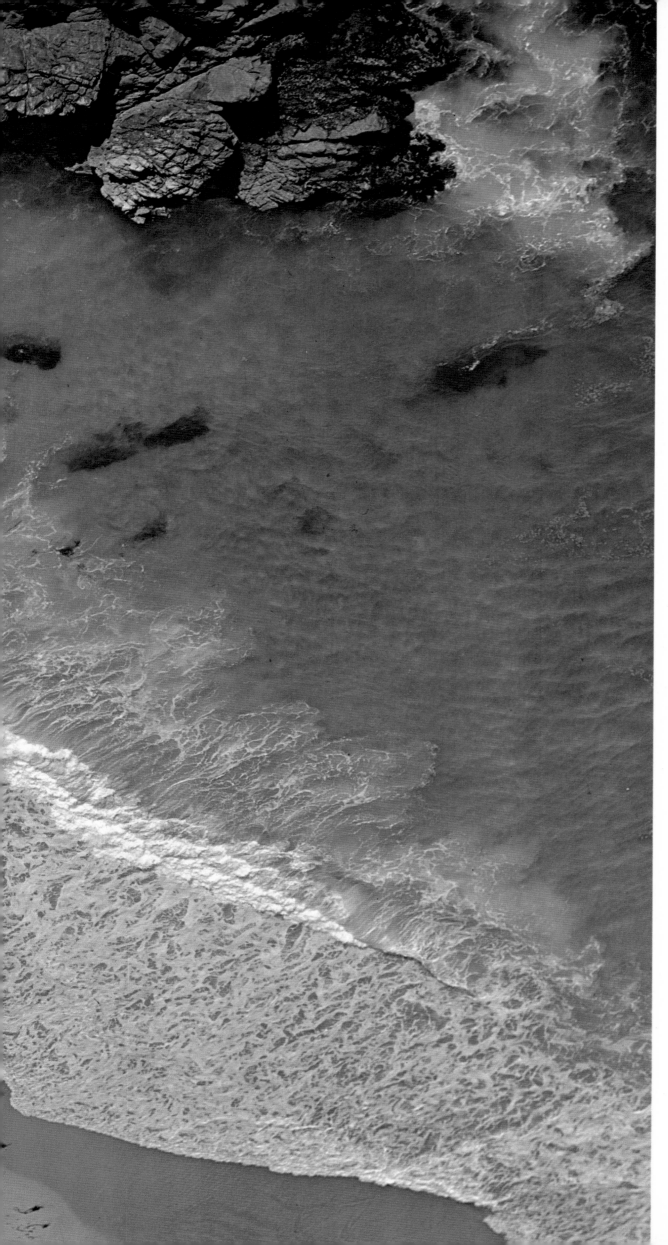

William Garnett: *Surf*

[81

WILLIAM GARNETT: *Surf*

WILLIAM GARNETT: *Surf*

The beaked and winged effluence
Felt the air foam under its throat and saw
The mountain sun-cup Tassajara, where fawns
Dance in the steam of the hot fountains at dawn,
Smoothed out, and the high strained ridges beyond Cachagua,
Where the rivers are born and the last condor is dead,
Flatten, and a hundred miles toward morning the Sierras
Dawn with their peaks of snow, and dwindle and smooth down
On the globed earth.

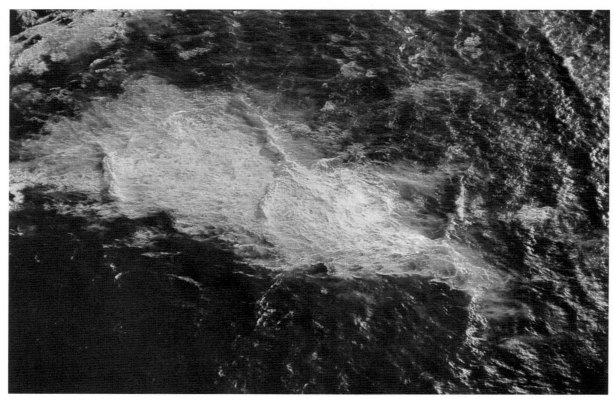

WILLIAM GARNETT: *Surf, Carmel*

It saw from the height and desert space
             of unbreathable air
Where meteors make green fire and die, the ocean dropping
             westward to the girdle of the pearls of dawn
And the hinder edge of the night sliding toward Asia;
             it saw far under eastward the April-delighted
Continent; and time relaxing about it now, abstracted from being,
             it saw the eagles destroyed,
Mean generations of gulls and crows taking their world:
             turn for turn in the air, as on earth
The white faces drove out the brown. It saw the white decayed
             and the brown from Asia returning;
It saw men learn to outfly the hawk's brood and forget it again;
             it saw men cover the earth and again
Devour each other and hide in caverns, be scarce as wolves. It neither
             wondered nor cared, and it saw
Growth and decay alternate forever, and the tides returning.

It saw, according to the sight of its kind, the archetype
Body of life a beaked carnivorous desire
Self-upheld on storm-broad wings: but the eyes
Were spouts of blood; the eyes were gashed out; dark blood
Ran from the ruinous eye-pits to the hook of the beak
And rained on the waste spaces of empty heaven.
Yet the great Life continued; yet the great Life
Was beautiful, and she drank her defeat, and devoured
Her famine for food.

             There the eagle's phantom perceived
Its prison and its wound were not its peculiar wretchedness,
All that lives was maimed and bleeding, caged or in blindness,
Lopped at the ends with death and conception, and shrewd
Cautery of pain on the stumps to stifle the blood, but not
Refrains for all that; life was more than its functions
And accidents, more important than its pains and pleasures,
A torch to burn in with pride, a necessary
Ecstasy in the run of the cold substance,
And scape-goat of the greater world. (But as for me,
I have heard the summer dust crying to be born
As much as ever flesh cried to be quiet.)
Pouring itself on fulfilment the eagle's passion
Left life behind and flew at the sun, its father.
The great unreal talons took peace for prey
Exultantly, their death beyond death; stooped upward, and struck
Peace like a white fawn in a dell of fire.

2. The Broken Balance

Mourning the broken balance, the hopeless prostration
of the earth
Under men's hands and their minds,
The beautiful places killed like rabbits to make a
city . . .

Man, introverted man, having crossed
In passage and but a little with the nature of things this
latter century
Has begot giants; but being taken up
Like a maniac with self-love and inward conflicts cannot
manage his hybrids.
Being used to deal with edgeless dreams,
Now he's bred knives on nature turns them also inward:
they have thirsty points though.
His mind forebodes his own destruction;
Actaeon who saw the goddess naked among leaves
and his hounds tore him.
A little knowledge, a pebble from the shingle,
A drop from the oceans: who would have dreamed this
infinitely little too much?

. . . They have done what never was done before. Not as a people
    takes a land to love it and be fed,
A little, according to need and love, and again a little; sparing
    the country tribes, mixing
Their blood with theirs, their minds with all the rocks and rivers,
    their flesh with the soil; no, without hunger
Wasting the world and your own labor, without love possessing,
    not even your hands to the dirt but plows
Like blades of knives; heartless machines; houses of steel: using
    and despising the patient earth . . .
Oh, as a rich man eats a forest for profit and a field for vanity,
    so you came west and raped
The continent and brushed its people to death. Without need,
    the weak skirmishing hunters, and without mercy. . . .

Ansel Adams: *Burned snag, former homestead near Scotia*

PASSENGER PIGEONS

Slowly the passenger pigeons increased, then suddenly
    their numbers
Became enormous, they would flatten ten miles of forest
When they flew down to roost, and the cloud of their rising
Eclipsed the dawns. They became too many, they are all dead,
Not one remains.
               And the American bison: their hordes
Would hide a prairie from horizon to horizon,
    great heads and storm-cloud shoulders, a torrent of life—
How many are left? For a time, for a few years, their bones
Turned the dark prairies white.
             You, Death, you watch
    for these things,
These explosions of life: they are your food,
They make your feasts.
             But turn your great rolling eyes
    away from humanity,
Those grossly craving black eyes. It is true we increase.
A man from Britain landing in Gaul when Rome
    had fallen,
He journeyed fourteen days inland through that beautiful
Rich land, the orchards and rivers and the looted villas:
    he reports that he saw
No living man. But now we fill up the gaps,

WILLIAM GARNETT: *Smog*

In spite of wars, famines and pestilences we are quite
    suddenly
Three billion people: our bones, ours too, would make
Wide prairies white, a beautiful snow of unburied bones:
Bones that have twitched and quivered in the nights of love,
Bones that have been shaken with laughter and hung slack
    in sorrow, coward bones
Worn out with trembling, strong bones broken on the rack,
    bones broken in battle,
Broad bones gnarled with hard labor, and the little bones
    of sweet young children, and the white empty skulls,
Little carved ivory wine-jugs that used to contain
Passion and thought and love and insane delirium, where now
Not even worms live.
                    Respect humanity, Death, these
    shameless black eyes of yours,
It is not necessary to take all at once—besides that,
    you cannot do it, we are too powerful,
We are men, not pigeons; you may take the old, the useless
    and helpless, the cancer-bitten and the tender young,
But the human race has still history to make. For look—
    look now
At our achievements: we have bridled the cloud-leaper lightning,
    a lion whipped by a man, to carry our messages
And work our will, we have snatched the live thunderbolt
Out of God's hands. Ha? That was little and last year—
    for now we have taken
The primal powers, creation and annihilation; we make
    new elements, such as God never saw,
We can explode atoms and annul the fragments, nothing left
    but pure energy, we shall use it
In peace and war—"Very clever," he answered,
    in his thin piping voice,
Cruel and a eunuch.

Roll those idiot black eyes of yours
On the field-beasts, not on intelligent man,
We are not in your order. You watched the dinosaurs
Grow into horror: they had been little efts in the ditches
    and presently became enormous, with leaping flanks
And tearing teeth, plated with armor, nothing could
    stand against them, nothing but you,
Death, and they died. You watched the sabre-tooth tigers
Develop those huge fangs, unnecessary as our sciences,
    and presently they died. You have their bones
In the oil-pits and layer-rock, you will not have ours.
    With pain and wonder and labor we have bought intelligence.
We have minds like the tusks of those forgotten tigers,
    hypertrophied and terrible,
We have counted the stars and half understood them,
    we have watched the farther galaxies fleeing away
    from us, wild herds
Of panic horses—or a trick of distance deceived the prism—
    we outfly falcons and eagles and meteors,
Faster than sound, higher than the nourishing air;
    we have enormous privilege, we do not fear you,
We have invented the jet-plane and the death-bomb
    and the cross of Christ—"Oh," he said, "surely
You'll live forever"—grinning like a skull, covering his mouth
    with his hand—"What could exterminate you?"

EDWARD WESTON: *Pelican*

THE PURSE-SEINE

Our sardine fishermen work at night in the dark of the moon;
       daylight or moonlight
They could not tell where to spread the net, unable to see
       the phosphorescence of the shoals of fish.
They work northward from Monterey, coasting Santa Cruz;
       off New Year's Point or off Pigeon Point
The look-out man will see some lakes of milk-color light on the
       sea's night-purple; he points, and the helmsman
Turns the dark prow, the motorboat circles the gleaming shoal
       and drifts out her seine-net. They close the circle
And purse the bottom of the net, then with great labor haul it in.

                          I cannot tell you
How beautiful the scene is, and a little terrible, then, when the
       crowded fish
Know they are caught, and wildly beat from one wall
       to the other of their closing destiny the phosphorescent
Water to a pool of flame, each beautiful slender body sheeted
       with flame, like a live rocket
A comet's tail wake of clear yellow flame; while outside
       the narrowing
Floats and cordage of the net great sea-lions come up to watch,
       sighing in the dark; the vast walls of night
Stand erect to the stars.

                   Lately I was looking from a night mountain-top
On a wide city, the colored splendor, galaxies of light: how could
       I help but recall the seine-net
Gathering the luminous fish? I cannot tell you how beautiful
       the city appeared, and a little terrible.
I thought, We have geared the machines and locked all together
       into interdependence; we have built the great cities; now
There is no escape. We have gathered vast populations incapable
       of free survival, insulated
From the strong earth, each person in himself helpless,
       on all dependent. The circle is closed, and the net
Is being hauled in. They hardly feel the cords drawing, yet
       they shine already. The inevitable mass-disasters
Will not come in our time nor in our children's, but we
       and our children
Must watch the net draw narrower, government take all powers—
       or revolution, and the new government
Take more than all, add to kept bodies kept souls—or anarchy,
       the mass-disasters.

These things are Progress;
Do you marvel our verse is troubled or frowning, while it keeps
	its reason? Or it lets go, lets the mood flow
In the manner of the recent young men into mere hysteria,
	splintered gleams, crackled laughter. But they are quite wrong.
There is no reason for amazement: surely one always knew
	that cultures decay, and life's end is death.

WILLIAM GARNETT: *Los Angeles*

Courtesy of the American Museum of Natural History:
The amphitheaters of Muyu-uray

"The contours of the architecture have been eroded by the elements, the site turned to pasture and farmland. . . . The largest theatre — probably set into a meteoric crater — accommodated as many as 60,000 people. . . . Nothing is known about the kind of spectacle performed . . ."

(the quotation is from *Architecture Without Architects*
by Bernard Rudofsky, Doubleday and Company, New York)

3. Human Again

At the fall of an age men must make sacrifice
To renew beauty, to restore strength.

SIGNPOST

Civilized, crying how to be human again: this will tell you how.
Turn outward, love things, not men, turn right away
     from humanity,
Let that doll lie. Consider if you like how the lilies grow,
Lean on the silent rock until you feel its divinity
Make your veins cold, look at the silent stars, let your eyes
Climb the great ladder out of the pit of yourself and man.
Things are so beautiful, your love will follow your eyes;
Things are the God, you will love God, and not in vain,
For what we love, we grow to it, we share its nature. At length
You will look back along the stars' rays and see that even
The poor doll humanity has a place under heaven.
Its qualities repair their mosaic around you, the chips of strength
And sickness; but now you are free, even to become human,
But born of the rock and the air, not of a woman.

CEDRIC WRIGHT: *Pacific, Autumn*

Men suffer want and become
Curiously ignoble; as prosperity
Made them curiously vile

But look how noble the world is,

STEVE CROUCH: *Coast and mist*

EDWARD WESTON: *Seaweed and Pacific*

The lonely-flowing waters,

Don Worth: *Foam*

Edward Weston: *Rock*

the secret-keeping stones,

ANSEL ADAMS: *Rock and shellfish*

CEDRIC WRIGHT: *Big Sur coast*

the flowing sky.

I entered the life of the brown forest,
And the great life of the ancient peaks, the patience of stone,

WYNN BULLOCK: *Forest*

Philip Hyde: *Falls in Anderson Creek Canyon*

I felt the changes in the veins
In the throat of the mountain,

and, I was the stream
Draining the mountain wood; and I the stag drinking;
        and I was the stars,
Boiling with light, wandering alone, each one the lord of his own summit;
        and I was the darkness
Outside the stars, I included them, they were a part of me.
        I was mankind also, a moving lichen
On the cheek of the round stone . . . they have not made words for it,
        to go behind things, beyond hours and ages,
And be all things in all time, in their returns and passages,
        in the motionless and timeless center,
In the white of the fire . . . how can I express the excellence
        I have found, that has no color but clearness;
No honey but ecstasy; nothing wrought nor remembered;
        no undertone nor silver second murmur
That rings in love's voice . . .

OH, LOVELY ROCK

We stayed the night in the pathless gorge of Ventana Creek,
    up the east fork.
The rock walls and the mountain ridges hung forest on forest
    above our heads, maple and redwood,
Laurel, oak, madrone, up to the high and slender Santa Lucian firs
    that stare up the cataracts
Of slide-rock to the star-color precipices.
                         We lay on gravel
    and kept a little camp-fire for warmth.
Past midnight only two or three coals glowed red in the cooling
    darkness; I laid a clutch of dead bay-leaves
On the ember ends and felted dry sticks across them
    and lay down again. The revived flame
Lighted my sleeping son's face and his companion's, and the vertical
    face of the great gorge-wall
Across the stream. Light leaves overhead danced in the fire's breath,
    tree-trunks were seen: it was the rock wall
That fascinated my eyes and mind. Nothing strange: light-gray
    diorite with two or three slanting seams in it,
Smooth-polished by the endless attrition of slides and floods;
    no fern nor lichen, pure naked rock . . . as if I were
Seeing rock for the first time. As if I were seeing through
    the flame-lit surface into the real and bodily
And living rock. Nothing strange . . . I cannot
Tell you how strange: the silent passion, the deep nobility
    and childlike loveliness: this fate going on
Outside our fates. It is here in the mountain like a grave
    smiling child. I shall die, and my boys
Will live and die, our world will go on through its rapid agonies
    of change and discovery; this age will die,
And wolves have howled in the snow around a new Bethlehem:
    this rock will be here, grave, earnest, not passive: the energies
That are its atoms will still be bearing the whole mountain above:
    and I, many packed centuries ago,
Felt its intense reality with love and wonder, this lonely rock.

STEVE CROUCH: *Boulders and stream*

SOLSTICE

Under this rain-wind the sombre magnificence of the coast
Remembers virtues older than Christ; I see
    the blood-brown wound of the river in the black bay,
The shark-tooth waves, the white gulls beaten
    on the black cloud, the streaming black rocks.
    Ah be strong, storm.

Pride and ferocity are virtues as well as love.
    I call to mind the dark mountains
    along the south,
The rock-heads in the cloud and the roaring cliffs,
    the redwoods cracking under the weight of wind,
These things wash clean the mind.
We even can face our lives, to bear them
    or change them. . . .

ROCK AND HAWK

Here is a symbol in which
Many high tragic thoughts
Watch their own eyes.

This gray rock, standing tall
On the headland, where the seawind
Lets no tree grow,

Earthquake-proved, and signatured
By ages of storms: on its peak
A falcon has perched.

I think, here is your emblem
To hang in the future sky;
Not the cross, not the hive,

But this; bright power, dark peace;
Fierce consciousness joined with final
Disinterestedness;

Life with calm death; the falcon's
Realist eyes and act
Married to the massive

Mysticism of stone,
Which failure cannot cast down
Nor success make proud.

ANSEL ADAMS: *Surf*

Morley Baer: *Ridges*

COMPENSATION

Solitude that unmakes me one of men
In snow-white hands brings singular recompense,
Evening me with kindlier natures when
On the needled pinewood the cold dews condense
About the hour of Rigel fallen from heaven
In wintertime, or when the long night tides
Sigh blindly from the sand-dune backward driven,
Or when on stormwings of the northwind rides
The foamscud with the cormorants, or when passes
A horse or dog with brown affectionate eyes,
Or autumn frosts are pricked by earliest grasses,
Or whirring from her covert a quail flies.
Why, even in humanity beauty and good
Show, from the mountainside of solitude.

BOATS IN A FOG

Sports and gallantries, the stage, the arts, the antics of dancers,
The exuberant voices of music,
Have charm for children but lack nobility; it is bitter earnestness
That makes beauty; the mind
Knows, grown adult.
                              A sudden fog-drift muffled the ocean,
A throbbing of engines moved in it,
At length, a stone's throw out, between the rocks and the vapor,
One by one moved shadows
Out of the mystery, shadows, fishing-boats, trailing each other
Following the cliff for guidance,
Holding a difficult path between the peril of the sea-fog
And the foam on the shore granite.
One by one, trailing their leader, six crept by me,
Out of the vapor and into it,
The throb of their engines subdued by the fog, patient and cautious,
Coasting all round the peninsula
Back to the buoys in Monterey harbor. A flight of pelicans
Is nothing lovelier to look at;
The flight of the planets is nothing nobler; all the arts lose virtue
Against the essential reality
Of creatures going about their business among the equally
Earnest elements of nature.

EDWARD WESTON: *Fishing Boat*

. . . Man gleaning food between the solemn presences of land
and ocean,
On shores where better men have shipwrecked, under fog
and among flowers,
Equals the mountains in his past and future . . .

CEDRIC WRIGHT: *South from Coastlands*

JERRY LEBECK: *Gulls*

. . . But chiefly the gulls, the cloud-calligraphers
        of windy spirals before a storm,
Cruise north and south over the sea-rocks and over
That bluish enormous opal; very lately these alone,
        these and the clouds
And westering lights of heaven . . .

. . . the great frame takes all creatures;
From the greatness of their element they all take beauty.

WYNN BULLOCK: *Fence and Bird*

THE BEAKS OF EAGLES

An eagle's nest on the head of an old redwood on one
     of the precipice-footed ridges
Above Ventana Creek, that jagged country which nothing
     but a falling meteor will ever plow; no horseman
Will ever ride there, no hunter cross this ridge but the winged ones,
     no one will steal the eggs from this fortress.
The she-eagle is old, her mate was shot long ago, she is now mated
     with a son of hers.
When lightning blasted her nest she built it again on the same tree,
     in the splinters of the thunderbolt.
The she-eagle is older than I; she was here when the fires
     of eighty-five raged on these ridges,
She was lately fledged and dared not hunt ahead of them but ate
     scorched meat. The world has changed in her time;
Humanity has multiplied, but not here; men's hopes and thoughts
     and customs have changed, their powers are enlarged,
Their powers and their follies have become fantastic,
The unstable animal never has been changed so rapidly. The motor
     and the plane and the great war have gone over him,
And Lenin has lived and Jehovah died: while the mother-eagle
Hunts her same hills, crying the same beautiful and lonely cry
     and is never tired; dreams the same dreams,
And hears at night the rock-slides rattle and thunder in the throats
     of these living mountains.
                  It is good for man
To try all changes, progress and corruption, powers, peace
     and anguish, not to go down the dinosaur's way
Until all his capacities have been explored: and it is good for him
To know that his needs and nature are no more changed in fact
     in ten thousand years than the beaks of eagles.

STEVE CROUCH: *Waterfall and mist*

CONTINENT'S END

At the equinox when the earth was veiled in a late rain, wreathed
  with wet poppies, waiting spring,
The ocean swelled for a far storm and beat its boundary,
  the ground-swell shook the beds of granite.

I gazing at the boundaries of granite and spray, the established
  sea-marks, felt behind me
Mountain and plain, the immense breadth of the continent,
  before me the mass and doubled stretch of water.

I said: You yoke the Aleutian seal-rocks with the lava and coral
  sowings that flower the south,
Over your flood the life that sought the sunrise faces ours that has
  followed the evening star.

The long migrations meet across you and it is nothing to you,
  you have forgotten us, mother.
You were much younger when we crawled out of the womb
  and lay in the sun's eye on the tideline.

It was long and long ago; we have grown proud since then
  and you have grown bitter; life retains
Your mobile soft unquiet strength; and envies hardness,
  the insolent quietness of stone.

The tides are in our veins, we still mirror the stars, life is your child,
  but there is in me
Older and harder than life and more impartial, the eye
  that watched before there was an ocean.

That watched you fill your beds out of the condensation of thin vapor
  and watched you change them,
That saw you soft and violent wear your boundaries down,
  eat rock, shift places with the continents.

Mother, though my song's measure is like your surf-beat's ancient
  rhythm I never learned it of you.
Before there was any water there were tides of fire, both our
  tones flow from the older fountain.

        . . . as if our blood had labored
  all around the earth from Asia
To play its mystery before strict judges at last, the final ocean
  and sky, to prove our nature
More shining than that of the other animals. It is rather ignoble
  in its quiet times, mean in its pleasures,
Slavish in the mass; but at stricken moments it can shine terribly
  against the dark magnificence of things.

STEVE CROUCH: *Headland and Pacific*

SLEVIN: *Hand prints*

HANDS

Inside a cave in a narrow canyon near Tassajara
The vault of rock is painted with hands,
A multitude of hands in the twilight, a cloud of men's palms,
    no more,
No other picture. There's no one to say
Whether the brown shy quiet people who are dead intended
Religion or magic, or made their tracings
In the idleness of art; but over the division of years these careful
Signs-manual are now like a sealed message
Saying: "Look: we also were human; we had hands, not paws.
    All hail
You people with the cleverer hands, our supplanters
In the beautiful country; enjoy her a season, her beauty,
    and come down
And be supplanted; for you also are human."

STEVE CROUCH: *Point Sur*

. . . I remember the farther
Future, and the last man dying
Without succession under the confident eyes of the stars.
It was only a moment's accident,
The race that plagued us; the world resumes the old lonely immortal
Splendor . . .

4. Flight of Swans

One who sees giant Orion, the torches of winter midnight,
Enormously walking above the ocean in the west of heaven;
And watches the track of this age of time at its peak of flight
Waver like a spent rocket, wavering toward new discoveries,
Mortal examinations of darkness, soundings of depth;
And watches the long coast mountain vibrate from bronze to green,
Bronze to green, year after year, and all the streams
Dry and flooded, dry and flooded, in the racing seasons;
And knows that exactly this and not another is the world,
The ideal is phantoms for bait, the spirit is a flicker on a grave;—
May serve, with a certain detachment, the fugitive human race,
Or his own people, or his own household; but hardly himself;
And will not wind himself into hopes nor sicken with despairs.
He has found the peace and adored the God; he handles in autumn
The germs of far-future spring.
                    Sad sons of the stormy fall,
No escape, you have to inflict and endure; surely it is time for you
To learn to touch the diamond within to the diamond outside,
Thinning your humanity a little between the invulnerable diamonds,
Knowing that your angry choices and hopes and terrors are in vain,
But life and death not in vain; and the world is like a flight of swans.

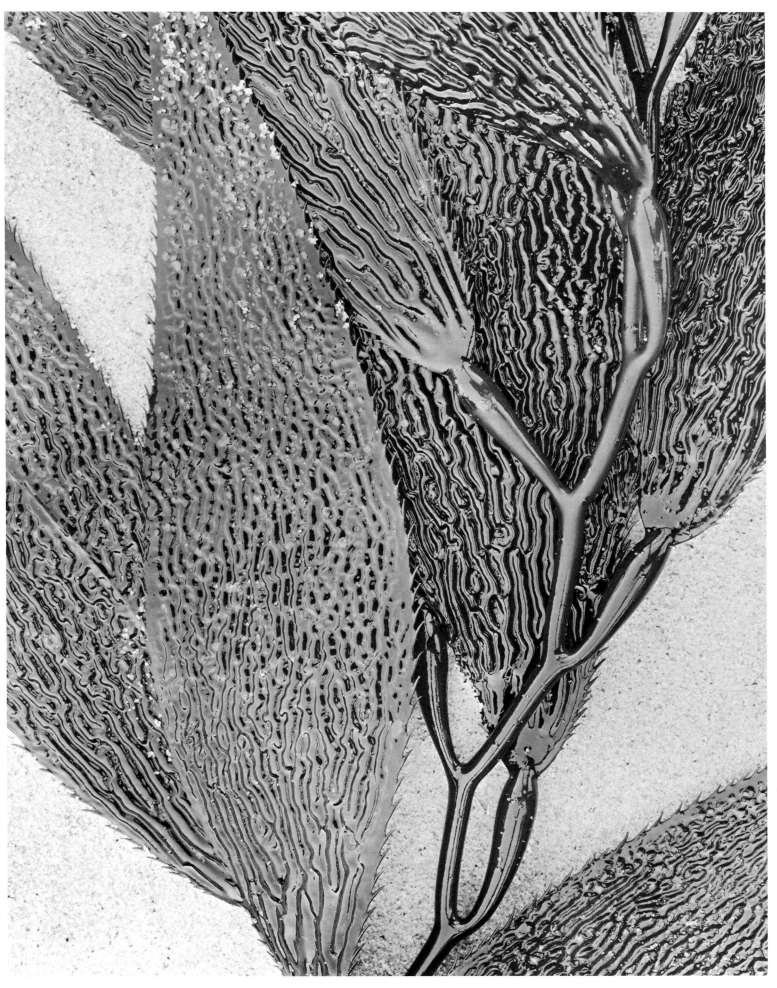

DON WORTH: *Kelp*

DON WORTH: *Pacific*

OCEAN

It dreams in the deepest sleep, it remembers the storm
    last month or it feels the far storm
Off Unalaska and the lash of the sea-rain.
It is never mournful but wise, and takes the magical
    misrule of the steep world
With strong tolerance, its depth is not moved
From where the green sun fails to where the thin red clay
    lies on the basalt
And there has never been light nor life.
The black crystal, the untroubled fountain, the roots of
    endurance.
                  Therefore I belted
The house and the tower and courtyard with stone,
And have planted the naked foreland with future forest
    toward noon and morning: for it told me,
The time I was gazing in the black crystal,
To be faithful in storm, patient of fools, tolerant of
    memories and the muttering prophets,
It is needful to have night in one's body.

OCTOBER EVENING

Male-throated under the shallow sea-fog
Moaned a ship's horn quivering the shorelong granite.
Coyotes toward the valley made answer,
Their little wolf-pads in the dead grass by the stream
Wet with the young season's first rain,
Their jagged wail trespassing among the steep stars.
What stars? Aldebaran under the dove-leash
Pleiades. I thought, in an hour Orion will be risen,
Be glad for summer is dead and the sky
Turns over to darkness, good storms, few guests, glad rivers.

STEVE CROUCH: *Storm clouds*

WYNN BULLOCK: *Beach and foam*

. . . There is the great and quiet water
Reaching to Asia, and in an hour or so
The still stars will show over it but I am quieter
Inside than even the ocean or the stars. . . .

STEVE CROUCH: *Sun and waves*

NIGHT

The ebb slips from the rock, the sunken
Tide-rocks lift streaming shoulders
Out of the slack, the slow west
Sombering its torch; a ship's light
Shows faintly, far out,
Over the weight of the prone ocean
On the low cloud.

Over the dark mountain, over the dark pinewood,
Down the long dark valley along the shrunken river,
Returns the splendor without rays, the shining of shadow,
Peace-bringer, the matrix of all shining and quieter of shining.
Where the shore widens on the bay she opens dark wings
And the ocean accepts her glory. O soul worshipful of her
You like the ocean have grave depths where she dwells always,
And the film of waves above that takes the sun takes also
Her, with more love. The sun-lovers have a blond favorite,
A father of lights and noises, wars, weeping and laughter,
Hot labor, lust and delight and the other blemishes. Quietness
Flows from her deeper fountain; and he will die; and she is immortal.

Far off from here the slender
Flocks of the mountain forest
Move among stems like towers
Of the old redwoods to the stream,
No twig crackling; dip shy
Wild muzzles into the mountain water
Among the dark ferns.

O passionately at peace you being secure will pardon
The blasphemies of glowworms, the lamp in my tower,
        the fretfulness
Of cities, the cressets of the planets, the pride of the stars.
This August night in a rift of cloud Antares reddens,
The great one, the ancient torch, a lord among lost children,
The earth's orbit doubled would not girdle his greatness, one fire
Globed, out of grasp of the mind enormous; but to you O Night
What? Not a spark? What flicker of a spark in the faint far glimmer
Of a lost fire dying in the desert, dim coals of a sand-pit the Bedouins
Wandered from at dawn . . . Ah singing prayer to what gulfs tempted
Suddenly are you more lost? To us the near-hand mountain
Be a measure of height, the tide-worn cliff at the sea-gate
        a measure of continuance.

The tide, moving the night's
Vastness with lonely voices,
Turns, the deep dark-shining
Pacific leans on the land,
Feeling his cold strength
To the outmost margins: you Night will resume
The stars in your time.

O passionately at peace when will that tide draw shoreward?
Truly the spouting fountains of light, Antares, Arcturus,
Tire of their flow, they sing one song but they think silence.
The striding winter giant Orion shines, and dreams darkness.
And life, the flicker of men and moths and the wolf on the hill,
Though furious for continuance, passionately feeding, passionately
Remaking itself upon its mates, remembers deep inward
The calm mother, the quietness of the womb and the egg,
The primal and the latter silences: dear Night it is memory
Prophesies, prophecy that remembers, the charm of the dark.
And I and my people, we are willing to love the four-score years
Heartily; but as a sailor loves the sea, when the helm is for harbor.

Have men's minds changed,
Or the rock hidden in the deep of the waters of the soul
Broken the surface? A few centuries
Gone by, was none dared not to people
The darkness beyond the stars with harps and habitations.
But now, dear is the truth. Life is grown sweeter and lonelier,
And death is no evil.

STEVE CROUCH: *Ridges and Pacific*

I admired the beauty
While I was human, now I am part of the beauty.
I wander in the air,
Being mostly gas and water, and flow in the ocean;
Touch you and Asia
At the same moment; have a hand in the sunrises
And the glow of this grass.
I left the light precipitate of ashes to earth
For a love-token.

EDWARD WESTON: *Cloud*

5. Return

THE DEER LAY DOWN THEIR BONES

I followed the narrow cliffside trail half way up the mountain
Above the deep river-canyon. There was a little cataract
    crossed the path, flinging itself
Over tree roots and rocks, shaking the jeweled fern-fronds, bright
    bubbling water
Pure from the mountain, but a bad smell came up. Wondering
    at it I clambered down the steep stream
Some forty feet, and found in the midst of bush-oak and laurel,
Hung like a bird's nest on the precipice brink a small hidden
    clearing,
Grass and a shallow pool. But all about there were bones
    lying in the grass, clean bones and stinking bones,
Antlers and bones: I understood that the place was
    a refuge for wounded deer; there are so many
Hurt ones escape the hunters and limp away to lie hidden; here
    they have water for the awful thirst
And peace to die in; dense green laurel and grim cliff
Make sanctuary, and a sweet wind blows upward from
    the deep gorge.—I wish my bones were with theirs.

STEVE CROUCH: *Forest floor*

But that's a foolish thing to confess, and a little cowardly. We
    know that life
Is on the whole quite equally good and bad, mostly gray neutral,
    and can be endured
To the dim end, no matter what magic of grass, water
    and precipice, and pain of wounds,
Makes death look dear. We have been given life and have used it—
    not a great gift perhaps—but in honesty
Should use it all. Mine's empty since my love died—Empty?
    The flame-haired grandchild with great blue eyes
That look like hers?—What can I do for the child? I gaze
    at her and wonder what sort of man
In the fall of the world . . . I am growing old, that is the trouble.
    My children and little grandchildren
Will find their way, and why should I wait ten years yet, having
    lived sixty-seven, ten years more or less,
Before I crawl out on a ledge of rock and die snapping, like a wolf
Who has lost his mate?—I am bound by my own
    thirty-year-old decision: who drinks the wine
Should take the dregs; even in the bitter lees and sediment
New discovery may lie. The deer in that beautiful place lay down
    their bones: I must wear mine.

EDWARD WESTON: *Broken cypress*

First draft of "Ocean"

I hate my verses, every line, every word.
Oh pale and brittle pencils ever to try
One grass-blade's curve, or the throat of one bird
That clings to twig, ruffled against white sky . . .

ELIOT PORTER: *Tern in flight*

Philip Hyde: *Cape Piedras Blancas*

SALVAGE

It is true that half the glory is gone.
Motors and modernist houses usurp the scene.
There is no eagle soaring, nor a puma
On the Carmel hill highroad, where thirty years ago
We watched one pass. Yet by God's grace
I have still a furlong of granite cliff, on which the Pacific
Leans his wild weight, and the trees I planted
When I was young, little green whips in hand,
Have grown in despite of the biting sea-wind,
And are accepted by nature, an angry-voiced tribe
    of night herons'
Nests on the boughs. One has to pay for it;
The county taxes take all my income, and it seems ridiculous
To hold three acres of shorelong woodland
And the little low house that my own hands made,
    at the annual cost
Of a shiny new car. Never mind, the trees and the stones
    are worth it.

Eliot Porter: *Osprey*

RETURN

A little too abstract, a little too wise,
It is time for us to kiss the earth again,
It is time to let the leaves rain from the skies,
Let the rich life run to the roots again.
I will go down to the lovely Sur Rivers
And dip my arms in them up to the shoulders.
I will find my accounting where the alder leaf quivers
In the ocean wind over the river boulders.
I will touch things and things and no more thoughts,
That breed like mouthless May-flies darkening the sky,
The insect clouds that blind our passionate hawks
So that they cannot strike, hardly can fly.
Things are the hawk's food and noble is the mountain, Oh noble
Pico Blanco, steep sea-wave of marble.

ILLUSTRATIONS